The Discovery Books are prepared

under the educational supervision of

Mary C. Austin, Ed. D.

Reading Specialist

and Lecturer on Education

Harvard University

A DISCOVERY BOOK

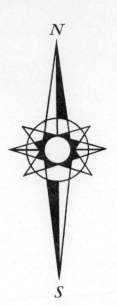

by Claire Huchet Bishop

illustrated by Maurice Brevannes

THE GARRARD PRESS

Champaign, Illinois

Lafayette

French-American Hero

TO MY FAITHFUL FRIEND
AND
SPIRITED TEACHER
CHARLOTTE HOMER

Contents

Lafayette:
French-American Hero

Chapter *1*

The Beast

"Gilbert! What are you doing? Come right down! At once!"

Gilbert, a tall, red-headed, eight-year-old boy, was standing on the back of a high chair. He was trying to reach a big sword which hung over the mantelpiece.

"Gilbert!"

He jumped down. "Grandmama," he cried, "please, take Papa's sword down for me!"

"Indeed not! What has come into your head, Gilbert?"

"Grandmama, you must give me the sword. There is an awful beast around. The village people are scared. Give me the sword, Grandmama. I will go into the forest and kill the beast!"

He waved his arms bravely. His grey-blue eyes were shining.

"I know all about the beast," Grandmama said. "Maybe it is a huge wolf. Nobody has set eyes on it yet."

"I will! I will! Give me the sword, Grandmama. Please!"

"I am going to send hunters after the beast. It is no work for you, Gilbert. But I am glad that you are so brave. One should be brave when one bears the name of Marie Joseph Paul Yves Roch Gilbert du Motier, Marquis de Lafayette."

Gilbert nodded. It was a long name. The last part of it always made him feel a little sad. Marquis was a French title for the head of a noble family. A marquis owned a lot of land. He was responsible for the welfare of hundreds of farmers, called peasants. Though he was so young Gilbert was already the head of the family. For his father had died on the battlefield before Gilbert was born on September 6, 1757.

For years, the Lafayettes had been soldiers in the army of the King of France. They did not have much money, but they were famous for their bravery.

Gilbert liked to hear about his ancestors. He kept asking his teacher, "Please, sir, tell me about that old Gilbert . . ."

"Your ancestor Gilbert was not old then. He fought with Joan of Arc, the French peasant girl who set France free from the English. His motto was . . ."

"Why not?" cried Gilbert.

"Yes, why not? In Latin it is cur non? And that is what is written on the Lafayettes' coat of arms."

"Why not?" shouted Gilbert. "When I grow up I will be a soldier too! Why not?"

Gilbert lived in the country with his grandmother and his aunt. Their house was the old family castle. It stood on a hill at Chavaniac, which is in the central part of France. The castle was a wonderful place to play hide and seek. There were huge dark rooms and long narrow halls with secret passages.

Gilbert's mother was away in Paris trying to plan his future. One day she came to Chavaniac and said, "Gilbert, we are going back to Paris to live with my father."

"But I don't want to leave Chavaniac!" cried Gilbert. "I love it here!"

"Don't you want to be a soldier?"

"Of course!"

"Then you have to go to school in Paris. Remember! You are a Lafayette!"

On his eleventh birthday his Grandmama and Auntie kissed Gilbert good-by. In the courtyard the peasants were waiting.

"Happy birthday and a safe journey to our Marquis!" they shouted.

Manfully, Gilbert kept his tears back, climbed into the coach and sat next to his mother.

Chapter 2

A Horse With Spirit

They were on the road several days. By the time they reached Paris, Gilbert had forgotten his sadness.

How exciting and noisy the city was! Soon they arrived at his grandfather's house. My! What a beautiful place it was! And all those servants in uniforms! Gilbert felt strange and shy, for he had never before met this grandfather.

At dinner that night Gilbert looked at all the forks, spoons and knives by his plate. Which one should he use?

He did not dare ask. Suddenly he
heard his grandfather's stern voice.

"Why don't you eat, boy?"

Gilbert was in a panic. But as he
looked up, his eyes met those of his
great-grandfather who was there too.
The old gentleman smiled kindly. All at
once Gilbert saw that he should use
the same fork his great-grandfather was
holding. He quickly picked it up.

School started a few days later. On the opening day Gilbert put on his school uniform. There was a navy blue suit trimmed with many colored braids and a little orange cap. Gilbert was in high spirits as he entered the school yard.

But to his surprise all the boys started laughing at him. They jumped up and down and shouted, "Look! Here comes Blondinette!" They called him Blondinette for his orange cap looked so funny on his red hair. This silly nickname stuck with him all his life.

But soon the boys began to like him. He made a special friend, Paul de Noailles.

One day Paul invited Gilbert to his cousin's, the Duke d'Ayen. He had a real palace right in Paris. The garden was large enough for hunting.

The Duke had five daughters. Gilbert and Paul played games with them in the garden. Gilbert was the captain and the others were soldiers. Adrienne d'Ayen was two years younger than Gilbert. She said to one of her sisters, "That Gilbert de Lafayette is more fun than any other boy I know."

Gilbert had good marks at school. One day the teacher asked the boys to write on the following subject — What do you think of a horse who throws a mean rider?

Gilbert did not hesitate. He wrote: *I like that horse. He is a horse with spirit. No one should abuse a horse. The horse was right to throw a mean rider.*

When Gilbert's grandfather heard about this he was furious.

"What do you mean?" he thundered. "Don't you know any better? A horse should obey. Even when he is abused, he should obey. What would the world come to if horses did not obey!"

Gilbert kept silent. But he said to himself, "I don't care. That horse was right. No one should be abused, not even a horse."

Soon after this a very sad thing happened. Gilbert's mother died. And a few weeks later his grandfather died too. Gilbert was now an orphan.

But the stern old gentleman left Gilbert all his money. So, in time, the poor boy of Chavaniac became one of the richest men in France.

Gilbert went to live with his great-grandfather. Later he entered military school at Versailles. Then Gilbert became a cadet in his grandfather's regiment, the Black Musketeers. They were the King's bodyguard.

When Gilbert rode horseback with the King's grandsons, people turned around to look at him. He was six feet tall and he wore a beautiful uniform. It was bright red and trimmed with gold. With his sword at his side, he would gallop along. What fun it was to show off!

Chapter 3

The American Farmers

When Gilbert was fourteen his great-grandfather told him he had found a suitable wife for him. Gilbert was not surprised. It was the custom to marry young in those days. Parents decided whom their children should marry.

Gilbert was pleased when he learned his future wife was the lovely Adrienne d'Ayen. Adrienne was happy too, for she liked Gilbert.

They were married two years later in Paris. It was spring. They looked like a fairy-tale couple under the pink and white blossoms of the chestnut trees.

The young King of France, Louis the Sixteenth, had just been married too. He and his wife Marie-Antoinette were not much older than the Lafayettes. So they asked them to lots of parties. They played outdoor games too. The most popular was hunt-the-fox. Gilbert was always "it" on account of his red hair.

But Gilbert did not like all the fancy plays and dances. Luckily he was soon able to leave Paris. Gilbert was captain of a regiment that was ordered to camp on the eastern border of France.

While he was there Gilbert went to a dinner which changed his whole life.

France and England had fought each other for hundreds of years.

At that time, the war had been called off. The Duke of Gloucester, brother of the King of England, took a trip around Europe. The officers of Gilbert's regiment gave a dinner in his honor.

At the dinner the Duke of Gloucester said, "My brother is having trouble with the people in his American colonies."

"What about, Your Highness?" asked Gilbert.

"It looks like war — a revolution."

A revolution! Everybody gasped.

"Yes. Those American Colonists think that they should not pay taxes on things they buy from England. They argue they did not have anything to say about the taxes. The Colonists call it taxation without representation.

They want to be free from England and govern themselves. Fancy!" The Duke chuckled.

Someone asked, "Does that mean that those people simply refuse to buy English goods?"

"That's right. Take tea, for instance. The American Colonists drink a lot of it. So my brother put a large tax on it. Recently an English ship arrived in Boston, loaded with tea. It was boarded by a lot of wild, almost naked Indians . . ."

"Indians!" Everybody stopped eating.

"Yes, Indians who dumped all the boxes of tea in the harbor. But those Indians were not Indians. They were Colonists dressed as Indians."

Everybody roared with laughter.

"You laugh," went on the Duke, "but my brother, the King, was angry. He sent soldiers to stop the fighting. Then, the most extraordinary thing happened. Why those American farmers defeated the English soldiers in a battle at a place called Bunker Hill." The Duke added, "Of course, that Bunker Hill victory was just luck. Those American Colonists do not have a chance."

Gilbert, whose father had been killed by English soldiers, could hardly hide his satisfaction.

"Your Highness," he asked, "who is the leader of the American soldiers?"

"A man by the name of George Washington."

George Washington? No one had ever heard his name before.

26

Chapter 4

Absent Without Leave

Gilbert wrote about that dinner to his wife. He said, *I feel great enthusiasm for the cause of those Americans. For it is right to rebel against injustice.*

He wanted very much to go and help the Americans. He persuaded his friend, Paul de Noailles, who had married Adrienne's sister, to go too.

They asked for a leave from the Army. They could not get it. So together, they went to their father-in-law in Paris to ask if he could help them. But the Duke was angry.

"What!" he cried. "Are you mad? If you try such foolishness, I'll have you arrested and thrown into prison!"

Paul gave up, but Gilbert did not. Secretly he went to see Mr. Deane, an American. Mr. Deane had been sent to Paris to try to get some help from the King of France. But the King was not interested.

"Marquis," said Mr. Deane, "I appreciate your offer. But the trouble is we cannot afford it."

"I don't want any pay."

"That's better. But even so, I have no way to get you to America."

"I will buy a ship, WHY NOT?"

Gilbert did find a ship. He bought it secretly. He also found some volunteers to go with him.

At last everything was ready. Mr. Deane gave him a letter introducing him to Congress.

Gilbert was excited but also very upset. He had to run away from the Army and become absent without leave. What a dishonorable thing for an officer to do! But Gilbert said to himself, *My honor is with the Americans.*

He dared not say good-by to his young wife for fear his plan might be discovered. He jumped in his coach. His horses had to race five hundred miles to the coast where his ship was waiting.

He was almost there when he learned that his father-in-law had sent the police to arrest him. They were not far behind.

"Stop!" cried Gilbert to his coachman. "Come down here!"

The coachman stepped down quickly. "Take off your uniform, we are going to exchange clothes," ordered Gilbert.

A few minutes later Gilbert was holding the reins and shouting to the horses. The coachman, dressed as a Marquis, sat inside the coach.

Soon Gilbert could see that the horses were tired. He would have to find fresh horses. They neared an inn. Gilbert brought the horses to a sharp stop. A girl came out of the house.

"Please, will you do me a favor?" asked Gilbert. "If the police come looking for a young man in a coach, tell them you have not seen anyone. Understand?"

The girl nodded. Gilbert led the horses behind the inn. Then he went to the stable and hid in the hay.

He had not been there long when he heard loud shouts outside and the trampling of horses. The police!

"Hey, girl! Have you seen a young man in a coach?"

"Yes, yes! A little while ago. He went that way!"

And the girl pointed to a road away from the coast.

Gilbert heard the horses galloping away. He waited for a while. Then he came out. But he did not dare take his coach again. Instead he took a horse and rode like the wind to his ship, *La Victoire,* the Victory.

"Sail at once!" he ordered.

Young Marquis de Lafayette was on his way to America.

Chapter *5*

Strange Welcome

Gilbert had never been on a ship before. He was seasick for days. When he felt better he spent his time learning English.

After forty-five days at sea his ship finally reached South Carolina. They had to be very careful not to be caught by English warships. So *La Victoire* sailed up the American coast to a small quiet harbor.

Lafayette and some men got in a rowboat and started for shore. Some friendly Negro fishermen took them

to a nearby plantation, or farm. The
plantation owner sent them to the city
of Charleston where they got a big
welcome. Then Lafayette went overland
to Philadelphia, the capital of the
new government.

As soon as he reached Philadelphia,
Lafayette tried to see the important men
in the government. He had Mr. Deane's
letter with him. But everyone was too
busy.

Mr. Lowell was the man in the new government who knew about foreign affairs. Lafayette met him in the street and stopped to talk to him. Mr. Lowell took one look at Lafayette and said,

"Mr. de Lafayette, you and your friends are nothing but a set of adventurers. That letter from Silas Deane does not mean a thing . . . We have not invited you to come. Gentlemen, I wish you good morning."

And with that Mr. Lowell walked away.

What a blow! But Lafayette would not give up. "They don't understand," he said. He went back to his inn, dipped his quill pen in ink and wrote to Congress.

I do not want any pay, and I want to serve as a volunteer.

What? No money? Congress sat up and took notice. Just then, a letter arrived from Silas Deane and Benjamin Franklin who was also in Paris. It told Congress all about Lafayette, his wealth, his famous family and the great help he could be to the Americans.

And to think they had greeted him so badly! An official hurried to his inn and offered him the rank of major-general, without pay.

Lafayette was delighted.

Next day he was invited to a dinner in General George Washington's honor.

Lafayette's heart beat fast as he crossed the room to meet Washington. Here was another man with money and a good education who had chosen to defend his fellow man's freedom.

Washington was old enough to be Lafayette's father. How grand and dignified he looked!

As the younger man approached, General Washington gave him a grave and steady look.

"Mr. de Lafayette," he said, "I should like to have you with me tomorrow to review the troops."

Next day, Lafayette and Washington stood facing the untrained, poorly-equipped American Army. It was made up of men who had just left their homes to free their country. Lafayette was silent. At last Washington said,

"We are rather embarrassed to show ourselves to an officer from France."

"I am here, Sir, to learn, not to teach," answered Lafayette quickly.

Chapter 6

Wounded

Lafayette had to learn fast.

There was fighting near Philadelphia. Washington's troops were overpowered and some began to run away.

"Can I join the battle, my dear General?" asked Lafayette.

Washington agreed and Gilbert dashed ahead. It was his first battle, but he was not afraid. He shouted and yelled and pushed ahead. Suddenly he found himself surrounded by Englishmen. Quickly he slipped from his horse.

He drew his sword and began fighting right and left.

All at once he felt faint. The nearest American soldier rushed up to him and helped him back on his horse. Blood was pouring from a wound on his leg. He managed to get away, however, and to ride to Washington's camp.

As soon as Washington saw young Lafayette he called his own doctor. *"Treat him as though he were my son,"* Washington said. Lafayette stayed at a farm while his wound healed. But he was impatient to fight again. He went back into the Army even before he could wear his boots. One of the officers wrote to Washington:

The Marquis is determined to be in the way of danger.

In turn Washington wrote to Congress:

Mr. de Lafayette possesses uncommon military talents, is of quick and sound judgement . . .

Congress decided that Lafayette could command some troops of his own.

"What troops would you choose?" asked Washington.

"My dear General, I thank you. The Virginia troops, please, I choose."

He was only twenty and already in command of a part of the American Army.

Chapter 7

A Great Day

Washington's army spent the next winter at Valley Forge. It was a very cold winter. They did not have enough warm clothes and they did not have enough to eat.

Lafayette shared the same hardships. One very cold night he gave his blanket to a soldier. The troops called him *the Soldiers' Friend.*

Washington liked the Frenchman more and more. He found him a fine leader and a great help. One day he called Lafayette for a special mission.

"Go and make friends with the Iroquois Indians. Try to stop them from helping the English," he said.

Lafayette's trip was a great success. The Indians liked him so much they adopted him into their tribe. They gave him the name of Kayewla. Fifty of them came back with him to help Washington.

All that long, cold winter Lafayette sent many letters to France urging the French to help the Americans.

Many Frenchmen wanted to help. They thought the Americans were right to want a vote in their own government. They thought everyone, everywhere, should help govern themselves.

One day in May, Lafayette received a letter from France. He read it quickly.

Then he rushed out of his tent to see Washington. He hugged the older man in his arms.

"My dear General!" Lafayette shouted. "The French are coming!"

Lafayette was so happy that he cried.

Four months before, a Treaty of Friendship had been signed in Paris between America and France. But there was no radio or telephone then. It had taken four months for the ships to carry the good news to America.

"Tomorrow I shall review the troops," said Washington. "General Lafayette, I will be most honored if you will join me."

The next day, they stood side by side to review the entire army.

After the review there was a huge party to celebrate the French-American treaty. France was the first foreign ally America had ever had.

Chapter 8

How The Plan Worked

The French were coming. But in the meanwhile the American soldiers had to continue fighting.

Washington called Lafayette. "Find out what the English are doing near Philadelphia."

Lafayette left with two thousand men. Among them were some of the Iroquois Indians.

But the English learned they were coming. General Howe rubbed his hands happily. "Now I will catch that boy!" He was very sure of himself.

So he planned a big party. He sent around invitations to meet General Marquis de Lafayette.

Meanwhile Lafayette was on his way. The country was strangely quiet! Lafayette feared something was wrong. He sent out some scouts.

The scouts reported that some German troops the English had hired were waiting ahead at the river. And the English were blocking the retreat at the crossroads behind.

"I am trapped!" thought Lafayette. Quickly he gave orders. "My Iroquois brothers will go ahead and amuse the Germans. The rest of you follow me."

The Indians went ahead. They hid behind trees and bushes on a hill above the river. Suddenly they all jumped

into view and gave fearful shrieks and
yells. They had war paint on their
bodies and bright feathers on their heads.
The Germans had never seen anything
like this before. They were so scared
they ran away.

But the Iroquois ran too. They had never seen soldiers like the Germans. They wore high bearskin hats, and their mustaches were dyed bright red.

Meantime Lafayette led his men cross-country. They circled behind the road where the English were waiting. Finally they were safely back at head-quarters. So were the Indians. The English did not have their party.

In July, the first French ships arrived. What a joy!

Helped by the French Navy, Lafayette and the French-American Army fought to free Newport, Rhode Island. But a terrible storm came up, and the French ships were badly hurt. They had to be taken to Boston for repairs.

The war was at a standstill. Lafayette could not rest until it was won. He could see that the Americans needed more money, more supplies and more trained men. He went to see Washington.

"My dear General, I should like to go to France for a short time. I believe I can tell the French how they can aid America."

"Go, my son. That may be the way you can serve America best."

Chapter *9*

A Beautiful Christmas

Lafayette sailed home on an American ship. In the French harbor the cannon boomed to welcome the first American flag.

Lafayette hurried to see the King. He asked him to help defeat the English quickly. The King liked the idea very much.

Suddenly the King of France frowned. "Now, about your absence without leave, two years ago," he said. "You'll have to be punished. You'll have to go to prison."

To prison! Lafayette was stunned.

"Yes," continued the King. "You will be imprisoned for a whole week . . . in your own home."

Lafayette hurried joyfully to his prison!

"My dear heart!" he cried as he held his lovely young wife in his arms.

"And here is your little Anastasia," said Adrienne. She pointed proudly to the baby girl who had been born just after Lafayette had sailed for America. "And Anastasia knows a few English words already!"

After his week in "prison" Lafayette called on Benjamin Franklin. Benjamin Franklin gave Lafayette a sword as a present from Congress. On the sword was Lafayette's motto, WHY NOT?

Also on the sword were the names of the famous battles he had fought in America.

For months everybody made a great fuss over Gilbert. He enjoyed this. In spite of his greatness he was a little vain. However he never forgot America's freedom. He kept talking about it and asking help from everybody.

Lafayette bought helmets, topped with red and black horse hair plumes, for his Virginia soldiers.

What a year, and what a beautiful Christmas! On Christmas eve a baby boy was born to the Lafayettes. "He shall be called George Washington, Marquis de Lafayette," announced Gilbert.

In April, Lafayette returned to America. He had brought with him as many volunteer soldiers as he could put on the ship.

He hurried to Washington's tent. "My dear General, my dear General! I have a son! And he has your name." The grave general smiled briefly.

"And help is coming: money, guns, more supplies, more soldiers and more French ships!"

"It is just in time, my son. We are in desperate need. There is no food, no clothing. Many men have deserted. I have only six thousand left. Go, my son, and speak to Congress."

Lafayette's good news gave the Americans new hope. They began to work hard again to win the war.

Chapter *10*

Victory

Late that summer some of the French ships arrived. The ships were commanded by General Rochambeau.

The French soldiers began to go ashore. Suddenly a voice called, "Hey, Blondinette!" It was Paul de Noailles!

Lafayette was delighted to see Paul. He wanted to put him and the French soldiers right to work. But Rochambeau thought it best to wait for the rest of the ships that were bringing more men and supplies.

They waited for the ships all autumn, and they waited all winter. They did not know that English warships had blocked the French harbor. No French ships had been able to sail.

Lafayette hated to wait. Finally Washington gave him something to do. "March your men down to Virginia. Our soldiers there need help badly. Hurry."

When Lafayette arrived in Virginia, he saw that the American Army there was not strong enough to win from the English. They needed the French ships to help them from the sea. But the French ships had not arrived.

What could Lafayette do?

How about playing his old game of hunt-the-fox with the English? He did.

He and his men ran back and forth across the country like foxes. The English chased them but never caught them. The English were furious.

Then some troops, coming to help Lafayette, got into a battle with the English. The Americans were badly outnumbered. Lafayette and his men dashed to the rescue. Lafayette's horse was shot from under him. Lafayette leaped on another horse and continued to fight. That second horse was killed too. Again Lafayette jumped on another horse and rallied his men around him. They fought bravely, and the English retreated to Yorktown.

Washington sent good news to Lafayette. Other French warships had come and were on their way to Yorktown.

Washington was marching to Virginia with the French generals and a large French-American Army. The English were bottled up!

The English ships attacked the French ships. But they were defeated. The French ships guarded the harbor and prevented the English in Yorktown from getting help. That made it easy for Washington to attack by land. The English fought for two days, but they knew it was hopeless.

Finally the English raised the white flag of surrender. In reply, the lace handkerchief of Paul de Noailles was waved on the American side.

The English marched out of York-town.

Washington had given strict orders to his troops and to the town people. They were not to make fun of, or laugh at the English. The English were defeated, but they had fought bravely.

When the English reached the field where the Americans and the French were waiting, there was complete silence. They laid down their arms and marched off, prisoners-of-war.

Yorktown was a great victory for the American side. However, the war was not yet at an end.

Lafayette went back to France to get more money. But, a few weeks later, England asked for peace.

A treaty was signed in France, on January 20, 1782.

Lafayette wrote to Washington:

I rejoice with you, my dear General, in this peace which fulfills all my desire . . .

Chapter *11*

The National Guest

Lafayette had helped America win her freedom. He was only twenty-four, yet he was already famous. He liked being famous, but that was not enough. He wanted everybody to be free.

Back in Paris Lafayette did not have to wait long to find people to free. The French too, wanted freedom.

They did not have to free themselves from a far-away king as the Americans had had to do. They had to fight their own king right at home.

Lafayette became one of the leaders

of the French Revolution. Everybody cheered him as he rode around on a prancing white horse. But during the bitter fight he was captured and put in prison.

When the war was over Lafayette got out of prison. The new government was not as good as he had hoped it would be. But he was not discouraged. For years he worked hard to make France strong and free.

Meanwhile Lafayette never forgot America. He had named his youngest daughter Virginia, for the State of Virginia. Through the years he kept writing to his American friends and sending them presents.

The Americans never forgot Lafayette either. They too wrote and sent gifts.

Finally, in 1824, when Lafayette was quite an old man, they sent him a very special letter. It was an invitation to come and visit America!

When Lafayette's ship came into New York harbor, the noise was deafening. The cannon boomed, horns tooted, bands played, people shouted. Boats and piers were gaily decorated.

Lafayette stepped off the ship onto a carpet that stretched all the way to the street. The crowd went wild with joy. "He is the last general left alive who fought in the American Revolution!" they said to each other.

Thousands of soldiers were waiting. Lafayette reviewed the American troops. Then he rode in a carriage in a huge parade. The people enjoyed a holiday.

Schools, shops and offices were closed. People crowded the streets. They hung from windows and roofs. Everybody cheered wildly.

For hours Lafayette waved at the crowds and shook hands. He heard someone say, "How well he speaks English!"

"And why should I not," replied Lafayette quickly, *"being an American just returned from a long visit to Europe!"*

That night there were fireworks. People danced and sang in the streets. The celebration lasted four days.

Lafayette had only one hundred days to visit all the states.

"It's impossible," people said. "You cannot do it in such a short time."

"And WHY NOT?" asked Lafayette.

He did it. He went by horse and carriage and by river boat. Often he traveled at night, by torchlight. People lined the roads at all hours. Thousands and thousands of children waited to see him. Soon carts had to follow him to carry all the presents and letters he received.

He was overjoyed to see some of his old soldiers. They wore the red and black plumed helmets he had bought them.

He went to visit the Negro woman who had cooked for Washington and for him. She was very old and very poor. Lafayette arranged for her to own her house.

One night, on the Erie Canal, an Indian suddenly jumped aboard

his boat. "Where is Kayewla?" cried
the Indian. That was the name the
Iroquois had given Lafayette when they
adopted him. So Kayewla and his
Iroquois friend talked together. Then the
happy Indian jumped back onto shore
and disappeared in the woods.

Lafayette visited the battlefields where he had fought. He also laid the cornerstone of the monument at Bunker Hill. Lafayette remembered the dinner so long ago, when he first heard of Bunker Hill and the American Revolution.

He went to Mount Vernon and knelt at Washington's grave, calling him *the greatest and best of men.*

Finally Lafayette visited John Quincy Adams, the new President of the United States. There were many parties at the White House. Congress remembered that Lafayette had spent most of his fortune for America's freedom. Congress give him a present of $200,000 and a large piece of land.

Sadly, the National Guest said good-by:

"God bless the American people,
each of their states and the Federal
Government!
Accept this patriotic farewell of an
overflowing heart!"

* * *

Lafayette had many grandchildren and great grandchildren. By law, all his male descendants are citizens of the United States as well as of France.

Next to Washington, the American-born general, it was Lafayette, the French general, who did the most to defeat the English and to win for America her freedom. And he helped start the long-lasting friendship between the two countries.

America will never forget Gilbert, Marquis de Lafayette.

Other Books by
CLAIRE HUCHET BISHOP

THE FIVE CHINESE BROTHERS

THE FERRYMAN

THE MAN WHO LOST HIS HEAD

AUGUSTUS

PANCAKES-PARIS

BLUE SPRING FARM

CHRISTOPHER THE GIANT

BERNARD AND HIS DOGS

TWENTY AND TEN

MARTIN DE PORRES, HERO

ALL ALONE

HAPPY CHRISTMAS!

THE BIG LOOP

TOTO'S TRIUMPH